Cyberdanger and Internet Safety

Cyberdanger and Internet Safety

A Hot Issue

Jennifer Lawler

Enslow Publishers, Inc.

40 Industrial Road   PO Box 38
Box 398   Aldershot
Berkeley Heights, NJ 07922   Hants GU12 6BP
USA   UK

http://www.enslow.com

Library of Congress Cataloging-in-Publication Data

Lawler, Jennifer, 1965–
    Cyberdanger and Internet safety: a hot issue / Jennifer Lawler
       p. cm. — (Hot issues)
    Includes bibliographical references.
    Summary: Discusses how the Internet can be a potentially
dangerous place if misused and provides advice for using it in a
positive, safe, and enjoyable way.
    ISBN 0-7660-1368-5
    1. Internet (Computer network) and children—Juvenile
literature. 2. Internet (Computer network)—Safety measures
—Juvenile literature. 3. Safety education—Juvenile literature.
[1. Internet (Computer network)—Safety measures. 2. Safety.]
I. Title. II. Series.
HQ784.I58 L38   2000
025.04'028'9—dc21
                                      99-037013

Printed in the United States of America

10 9 8 7 6 5 4 3 2 1

To Our Readers:
All Internet addresses in this book were active and appropriate when we
went to press. Any comments or suggestions can be sent by e-mail to
Comments@enslow.com or to the address on the back cover.

Illustration Credits: AP/Wide World Photos, pp. 7, 11, 22, 27, 32,
36, 40, 52; © Corel Corporation, pp. 3, 6, 50; Skjold Photos, p. 20.

Cover Illustration: Image © 1995 PhotoDisc, Inc.

Contents

Not long ago, a teenage girl in New Jersey met a teenage boy on the Internet. At least, she thought she did. The two belonged to an online bulletin board—a place where people leave messages for each other about topics of interest to them. The boy said he was interested in having an e-mail pen pal, and the girl agreed that this would be fun.

She told him that she was thirteen years old. He said he was fifteen. A few months after they met online, he asked the girl to send him some photographs of herself, so she did. Later, after confessing how much he liked her, he asked her to send nude photographs of herself—which she did. Over the next few months, he encouraged her to send more. He even talked her into sending him videotapes of herself, with sexually explicit overtones.

When the girl's parents finally became suspicious of what she was doing and found out about the "pen pal," they contacted the police. The district attorney and the FBI investigated and learned that the "boy" was no boy. He was a forty-six-year-old man who conned the teenage girl into producing sexually explicit photographs of herself. At the man's sentencing, the girl called what had happened "emotional rape." Even several years later, she has trouble understanding how it happened and why her online friendship went wrong.

The prosecuting attorney for the case, Faith

Hochberg, says, "The sad lesson in this crime is the cruel manipulation and victimization of a young girl. [The crime] will continue to haunt her and her family for years to come." Hochberg went on to say,

> With the anonymity of online conversation, anyone can pretend to be anyone else. Over the years, we've warned our children to be wary of the strangers that they see. Now we must warn children . . . that the person they can't see sitting at the other keyboard could be a criminal pretending to be your friend.[1]

*S*gt. Rock, whose real name is not revealed because of death threats, looks for child pornography offenders on the Internet. He is a member of the Ethical Hackers Against Pedophilia. Pedophilia is a sexual attraction toward children.

Although this case is certainly not typical of what happens when people use the Internet, it illustrates one fear many people share: The Internet can be a dangerous place, and anyone can become a victim.

However, the Internet does not have to be a frightening, dangerous, or annoying place. In fact, it can be an exciting world full of information, exploration, and communication. More and more, it is becoming an essential tool in a complex world. If one learns how to use this tool wisely, Internet use can be safe and enjoyable.

Chapter 1

What Is the Internet?

The Internet is an international network that connects millions of computers so that computer users can share information and communicate with each other. It has been called the "information superhighway," since so much information flows through it.[1] Experts estimate that between 30 and 40 million Americans go online— meaning use the Internet—at least once a week.[2]

Using a computer, a special device called a modem, and a telephone or cable line, people can access the Internet. The World Wide Web, sometimes abbreviated "WWW" or called "the Web," is the system that allows computer users to present and retrieve information over the Internet. With the Web, users have an easier time finding the information they want.

On the Internet, computer users can visit information sites called Web pages or Web sites. They can join chat groups, which are places where people interested in the same hobbies and activities can talk online. People with shared interests carry on conversations, post information, and ask questions. People "talk" to each other by typing messages back and forth. In computer lingo, this is called "chatting in real time."[3] "Open" or "public" chat rooms allow many people to talk at once. Private chat rooms allow people to talk one-on-one.

By going online, people can also send electronic mail, called e-mail, to anyone else who has an e-mail address. E-mail works like a letter, only faster. A person sends a message to someone, who reads it, then can send a message back. No envelope, stamp, or running to the post office is needed.

Computer users also visit bulletin boards, which are special networks that are dialed directly. Bulletin boards are not always on the Internet itself, but they are used by Internet users. People post messages asking for information about a topic and read what other people have written. Bulletin boards are often used by computer companies to provide technical support. Users can even obtain software to make their computers run better, but electronically copying information from the Internet to one's computer (also called downloading) should always be done carefully to avoid getting bad files.

Newsgroups are similar to bulletin boards. They can be found on the Internet, in an area called UseNet. Thousands of newsgroups exist, covering a tremendous variety of subjects. Interested people subscribe to a group. Some require membership fees. A member who has signed up can post messages and reply to others. To join a newsgroup, you need a newsreader software program. People can also subscribe to a mailing list, sometimes called a list server, which provides members with information on a special topic of interest. These

*M*any young people know more about the Internet than adults do. Here, third-grader Anna Walter teaches an Internet class to adults at her school in Wichita, Kansas.

messages come directly to members' e-mail boxes. The mailing list sponsor may be a company, individual, or organization interested in providing information and encouraging the free exchange of ideas. Mailing lists can be created for almost any purpose. For example, people can subscribe to a mailing list that sends them a word and its definition each day.[4] Mailing list subscribers can send private e-mail messages to other subscribers. People who participate in bulletin-board services, newsgroups, and mailing lists do not have conversations that take place in real time.

How Is the Internet Accessed?

Computer users gain access to the Internet by using an Internet Service Provider (ISP). Usually ISPs also offer e-mail service to their customers. Some ISPs are run by the government, by schools, or by large businesses. Many other national, regional, and local companies also provide this service to subscribers for a monthly fee. Some companies, such as America Online, offer additional services. Such companies are called Internet portals. They provide a gateway to the Web and have member-only services and forums.

Typically, the computer uses a modem to send information over a phone line. The computer dials the phone number of the service provider's computer. The provider's computer, called a server, also has a modem. It answers the phone and establishes a connection between the customer's computer and the Internet. There are other ways to gain access to the Internet, but they all work in basically the same way. With a cable hookup, a local cable television company is the service provider. Cable access to the Internet requires a special cable modem. People can also use WebTV and digital satellite systems to gain access to the Internet. Both of these require regular phone lines in order for the user to request information. Many local phone companies also offer a special line that is dedicated for Internet use only. Called an Integrated Services Digital Network (ISDN), this is not a regular phone line but instead is a special connection able to send digital (computer) data without having to change it to analog (phone line) data. This increases the speed of transmission.[5] Another option is a T1 line, which is ten times faster than an ISDN line but costs thousands of dollars to install and operate.

Not all these methods are available in all areas, but they do have things in common. A person needs a computer or a special piece of computerlike equipment (like WebTV), a service provider (the cable company, an ISP, a local area network, or the phone company), and a line or cable to send data.

Once Internet service has been established, the computer user chooses a Web browser, such as Microsoft Internet Explorer or Netscape Navigator, which helps the computer interpret the data it receives and forms viewable pages of information. A Web user often chooses a search engine, too, such as Yahoo! or Alta Vista. A search engine helps organize the many Web sites (there are millions and millions of them—so many that no one has been able to come up with an accurate count). The engine helps users find Web pages without their having to know the address. Instead, users just type in a few descriptive words, called key words.[6] The search engine is a special Web site that has a list of thousands of Web pages organized by subject. When users type in keywords, the search engine lists the pages that match.

How Online Addresses Work

To visit a particular site on the Internet, you need the site's address. A search engine helps you find these Internet addresses, just as a phone book helps you find street addresses. All computers connected to the Internet have a specific Internet Protocol (IP) address, which is a unique series of numbers, such as 207.25.71.199. Since numbers are hard to remember, word addresses are also used. A site's

Domain Names and Organization Types

Domain	Used by	Example
com	businesses	nfl.com (National Football League)
edu	American educational institutions	yale.edu (Yale University)
gov	Unites States government	irs.gov (Internal Revenue Service)
int	International organizations	un.int (United Nations)
mil	United States military	army.mil (U.S. Army)
net	online service providers	idir.net (Internet Direct service provider)
org	private or nonprofit organizations	aclu.org (American Civil Liberties Union)

word address is interchangeable with its IP address. In a sense, the word address is like a nickname.

An address on the Web is called a Uniform Resource Locator (URL). The first part of the Web address tells the computer how the information should be sent. For most addresses, the first part is "http://," which stands for HyperText Transfer Protocol. But sometimes it might be "ftp://," which stands for File Transfer Protocol, or "telnet://," which stands for Telnet Protocol. Most browsers and search engines automatically insert "http://."[7]

The next part of the Web address says where the site will be found. For most Web addresses, this is the World Wide Web, so this part of the address is "www." If the Web address does not use the "www" indicator, it will use another indicator, such as "info."

The address then lists the name of the site, which might be the same as the name of the company, government agency, or person that sponsors the site, such as "fbi" or "disney." The last part of a Web address describes the type of organization sponsoring the site. This is called a domain. Businesses use "com," schools and colleges use "edu," the federal government uses "gov," and so on. These domains are not used outside the United States. Instead, a two-letter abbreviation for the country is used, such as "br" for Brazil, "jp" for Japan, and "uk" for the United Kingdom.[8] The different parts of the address are separated by periods, which are called dots in computer lingo. Thus, a Web address looks like this: http://www.fbi.gov. The entire address is called the registered domain name.

E-mail addresses, which are not the same as Web addresses, allow people to send and receive personal messages. E-mail is similar to regular postal mail, but it is sent through computers. Everyone who shares a computer can use the same address, so each person in a family or in a classroom group does not have to set up a separate e-mail account. However, outgoing and incoming messages will not be private.

E-mail addresses contain a username, which is the name the address owner uses to identify him- or herself, and the domain of the e-mail service. The username, sometimes called the user ID, can be anything. It does not have to be someone's name. In fact, to be safe, it is best to avoid using your own name. Instead, a person can use the name of a pet, the first five letters of the alphabet, or anything else that is easy to remember. One medical researcher uses "germ."[9] If two words make up the username, an underline separates them. Thus, a businessman who wants to use his whole name might have "joe_smith" as his e-mail username.

The next part of the e-mail address tells the computer where a person's messages are stored, usually on the Internet Service Provider's server. These two parts are separated by the symbol "@," which means "at." The last part is the domain or type of organization, usually "net" or "com." So an e-mail address might look like this: username@isp.net.[10]

Addresses are sometimes case sensitive, which means that if the address should appear in lowercase letters and it is typed in uppercase letters, the computer may not connect to the correct address.

Passwords and the Internet

The Internet can be accessed from computers at home, at school, and at the library. Depending on the type of Internet access, a person may have to use the same computer all the time to read e-mail messages. Sometimes a password is needed to go online or to use e-mail.

Always ask permission before using a computer to go online. Never give a personal password to anyone except parents, not even a best friend. When selecting a password, use something easy to remember, but hard to guess. That means not using birth dates or the names of family members. The longer and more random a password is, the better. The best password is a mix of letters and numbers. One person uses her dog's name—Dakota—so she can remember it, but she spells the name "duhkota" so that someone else could not guess it.[11]

How to Select an E-mail Password

- ✓ Do not select your name or the name of a family member or a pet.

- ✓ Do not use birthdates.

- ✓ Do not choose a real word.

- ✓ Use at least six characters.

- ✓ Combine letters with numbers.

- ✓ Use capital and lowercase letters.

Following these steps will help a person select a password that no one will be able to guess. Remember, do not write your password down anywhere and do not give it to anyone else, not even your best friend.

Source: *SafeKids.Com*, 1998, <http://www.safekids.com> (November 22, 1999).

Benefits of the Internet

The Internet has many exciting things on it. A student can get help with homework, look up information, play computer games with people across the country, and become a skilled computer user. People can improve their reading skills, communicate with others, and get involved with new hobbies. They can use the Internet to share classroom projects with people in other classrooms, collaborate on ideas, go shopping, find out about current events, or e-mail the White House.[12] People can get product information, technical support, even software. They can listen to music before buying it, read e-zines (online magazines), and look for a new job.

However, sometimes using the Internet can be unsafe, even dangerous. These dangers range from clever con artists, to violent criminals who lurk in chat rooms trying to find out a person's address. In order to protect oneself from all these dangers, a person must first be aware of them.

Chapter 2

How Can the Internet Be Unsafe?

The Internet appeals to people for many reasons. Some people like being able to look up information without going to the library. Others relax by visiting chat rooms and discussing current events. Still other people use the Internet mainly for e-mail, which they find is a quick and easy way to keep in touch with others. However, some people use the Internet for malicious or criminal activities.

Like the rest of the world, the Internet is made up of good and bad people. Yet because people are indoors at home or in school when they visit, the Internet can seem like a much safer place than the outside world. The Internet is not always safe, though. One of the reasons is that people think of computers as barriers that protect them.[1] They sometimes do things on the Internet they would never do in public, such as telling secrets or exchanging personal information.

Impersonation, harassment, stalking, fraud, illegal enticement—many crimes that occur in the real world can take place on the Internet. People on the

*M*any students use the vast resources of the Internet to get help with their homework.

Internet can also be exposed to obscene, violent, or otherwise inappropriate material, even if they are not seeking it.

Erica, a teenager, was visiting her grandparents' house with her mother. While there, she logged on to America Online (AOL). She went to a chat room and started talking with a boy who seemed very nice. They talked about their friends and hobbies. Then, her new friend asked if he could send Erica his picture over the Internet. Erica, flattered by his interest, said yes. In a few minutes, she received the picture—a snapshot of a completely naked man. Erica wisely called her mother, and they logged off, then told AOL what had happened. Erica certainly was not looking for this kind of material. Someone else simply took advantage of her.[2]

The most commonly reported Internet crimes are child pornography, fraud, e-mail abuse, and harassment.[3] Because of these concerns, many people want the government to control the kind of material available on the Internet. As a result, the Communications Decency Act of 1996 was enacted. In 1997, however, it was overturned by the United States Supreme Court. The act had attempted to restrict "indecent material" on the Internet.[4] The Supreme Court justices ruled that on the Internet it was impossible to prevent inappropriate material from reaching children and young adults without illegal censorship.

Even if the United States government could somehow control the material on the Internet, it would not be able to regulate material from other countries. Since the Internet connects people worldwide, Americans would still have to deal with inappropriate and illegal activities by people in other countries. This means that each individual user—not the government—is responsible for safely using the Internet.[5]

Since Internet activity is largely unrestricted, sometimes illegal or inappropriate behavior occurs. Because of the Internet's freewheeling atmosphere, it is easy to forget about being careful. Many annoyances and threats exist that all Internet visitors should know and watch out for.

People Can Hide Their Identities

The single most important fact to remember when using the Internet is that people online may not be who they say they are. For example Mike, a student, is interested in computer games. He joins a chat group to talk about a game that is supposed to be released in time for summer vacation. Another person in the chat group says she can hardly wait until the new game comes out. She says that she is a thirteen-year-old from Florida and asks Mike to tell her about himself.

Before Mike answers, he should think. How does he know she is really a thirteen-year-old? How does he even know she is really a girl? He does not. Mike has no way of finding out. Even the person's return e-mail address could be fake—he or she could be

*A*uthor Jean Armout Polly shows some students the new safety tools provided by Ameritech's Web site.

using a dummy e-mail account or a stolen one. People can visit anonymizer sites, where they are given an anonymous ID so that information cannot be collected about them.[6] They can also use a remailer. These services remove identifying information before sending an e-mail message on to the recipient. Anonymizers and remailers protect an Internet user's privacy, but they are also used by harassers. A harasser who uses them has little fear of being identified.

As Lawrence J. Magid, a syndicated columnist for *The Los Angeles Times*, puts it, "Just because you get a message from <grandma@cottage.com> doesn't mean it's really from grandma. It could really be from <wolf@bigfangs.com>."[7]

One Internet expert, Chris Peterson, cautions, "Don't count on any chat room participants being the gender, age, or anything else they claim. Such fooling occurs regularly in Internet conversations."[8]

Threatening or Obscene Material

Some Web sites, newsgroups, or other Internet areas can contain material or messages that might not be appropriate for young adults. A person does not always know when a chat group or Web site will have obscene material. A person might stumble across a hate group that has frightening ideas. A hate group is a group of people that encourages violence against and oppression of groups that are different from them, for reasons such as skin color, gender, religious preference, and the like. Many of them have begun using the Internet to spread their dangerous messages.

It is also possible to stumble across pornographic

material when one least expects it, although some experts dismiss this problem as having been exaggerated. Peter Kent, a computer systems expert, says, "The press has spent a lot of time over the past couple years talking about how the Internet is awash in pornography. . . . In general, you won't just trip over [it]."[9]

Although that may be true to some extent, users have found that some sites are designed to catch people who make a typing error. They mistype "Disney," "Infoseek," or one of several other common Web site addresses, and a porn site comes up.

Some people on the Internet enjoy threatening others or sending obscene messages. As Laura E. Quarantiello, a computer security expert, relates, "A reporter for *Computer Life* magazine once posed on the Internet as a 15-year-old cheerleader and got more than 30 messages of a sexual nature."[10] Although a person can just leave a Web site that has obscene material, it is harder to handle when threats or harassment are personally directed. To avoid such occurrences, use gender-neutral names. This means choosing a name like Pat that either a boy or a girl might have. Or just use initials. Do not reveal any personal information. If someone sends you a nasty or indecent message, be sure to tell your parents immediately.

Dangerous Internet Users

Some people on the Internet may want to hurt or exploit others. They may pretend to be a certain age with certain interests to gain the trust of another Internet visitor. Then they may try to talk that person into giving out their address or meeting with them. Such people might intend to hurt someone else.

Online Safety Pledge

✓ I will not give out personal information such as
  ➢ my name;
  ➢ my address and telephone number;
  ➢ my parents' workplace and telephone number;
  ➢ the name and location of my school.

✓ I will tell my parents if I come across anything that makes me feel uncomfortable.

✓ I will never arrange or agree to a face-to-face meeting with someone I met on the Internet. I will tell my parents if someone asks me to meet them.

✓ I will never send my picture or any information to someone online without my parents' permission.

✓ I will not respond to messages that make me feel uncomfortable or threatened. I will tell my parents if I receive such messages.

✓ I will talk with my parents about rules for going online.

✓ I will not enter contests or register for prizes without asking my parents first.

✓ I will check with my parents before downloading programs to my computer.

✓ I will always treat others on the Internet the way I would like to be treated.

Source: Lawrence J. Magid, "Child Safety on the Information Highway," *SafeKids.Com*, 1998, <http://www.safekids.com/child_safety.htm> (October 27, 1999).

Even if they do not want to hurt other people physically, they might try to steal from them or otherwise cause harm.

Although it happens rarely, dangerous Internet users can turn into stalkers. They begin with a test period of sending inappropriate or mean messages to see if they can provoke a response. A stalker wants a reaction, so refusing to respond to such messages can be the best way to stop this type of harassment from continuing.

Some disturbed people want to meet children and young adults in order to engage in illicit behavior, like taking nude photographs or engaging in sex acts. To put it bluntly, people who prey on children use the Internet to find victims. These people get to know children and young adults by browsing through messages left in a newsgroup or chat room. Then they begin to exchange frequent messages in order to gain the person's confidence. Their goal is personal contact with the user.[11] Do not make this contact.

Sometimes a criminal will masquerade as a child or young adult to gain the trust of other children and young adults. Once a relationship is established, the criminal will ask the user to meet an older friend. The criminal switches roles and plays this older friend, too. This role switching makes the older friend appear more trustworthy. After all, the friend was "introduced" by someone of the same age as the user.

Dangerous Group Participation

Another Internet user might try to encourage participation in activities that are illegal or inappropriate. People involved in cults sometimes

OUR POSITION AGAINST SUICIDE

We know that it is only while we are in these physical vehicles (bodies) that we can learn the lessons needed to complete our own individual transition, as well as to complete our task of offering the Kingdom of Heaven to this civilization one last time. We take good care of our vehicles so they can function well for us in this task, and we try to protect them from any harm.

We fully desire, expect, and look forward to boarding a spacecraft from the Next Level very soon (in our physical bodies). There is no doubt in our mind that our being "picked up" is inevitable in the very near future. But what happens between now and then is the **big question**. We are keenly aware of several possibilities.

It could happen that before that spacecraft comes, one or more of us could lose our physical vehicles (bodies) due to "recall," accident, or at the hands of some irate individual. We do not anticipate this, but it is possible. Another possibility is that, because of the position we take in our information, we could find so much disfavor with the powers that control this world that there could be attempts to incarcerate us or to subject us to some sort of psychological or physical torture (such as occurred at both Ruby Ridge and Waco).

It has always been our way to examine all possibilities, and be mentally prepared for whatever may come our way. For example, consider what happened at Masada around 73 A.D. A devout Jewish sect, after holding out against a siege by the Romans, to the best of their ability, and seeing that the murder, rape, and torture of their community was inevitable, determined that it was permissible for them to evacuate their bodies by a more dignified, and less agonizing method. We have thoroughly discussed this topic (of willful exit of the body under such conditions), and have mentally prepared ourselves for this possibility (as can be seen in a few of our statements). However, this act certainly does not need serious consideration at this time, and hopefully will not in the future.

The true meaning of "suicide" is *to turn against the Next Level when it is being offered.* In these last days, we are focused on two primary tasks: one - of making a last attempt at telling the truth about how the Next Level may be entered (our last effort at offering to individuals of this civilization the way to avoid "suicide"); and two - taking advantage of the rare opportunity we have each day - to work individually on our personal overcoming and change, in preparation for entering the Kingdom of Heaven.

This page from the Heaven's Gate Web site seems to state the cult's opposition to suicide. However, thirty-nine members of the cult actually did kill themselves.

use the Internet to acquire new members. Such groups want to make others feel as if they would be less lonely or happier if they joined the cult. The Heaven's Gate cult, whose leader and thirty-eight other members committed suicide in March 1997, used a Web page to attract new followers.

Other Internet users may want people to join them in computer hacking, as a challenge or a dare. Computer hackers get access to other people's computer systems, sometimes illegally, using special computer knowledge or computer tools. Sometimes hackers change or destroy information in other people's computer systems. This causes serious problems for business owners, the government, and other organizations, as well as for private individuals.

Hate groups sometimes try to earn people's sympathy on the internet. The Ku Klux Klan and the National Alliance, two racist groups, have found that Web sites and chat groups are an inexpensive way to try to convince people to accept their views. Hate groups use their Web sites to recruit members to their movements, using sophisticated sales techniques to interest people in their messages. The Simon Wiesenthal Center, which tracks such Web sites, reports that there are more than two thousand hate group Web sites in existence.[12]

Many young people are curious about dangerous things, but people they meet on the Internet may not only fantasize about sex or cults or dangerous activities but also carry out their fantasies.

Loss of Privacy

When people hop on the Internet, they can easily lose their privacy and the privacy of their family and friends. If a person sends an e-mail joke to a friend and he or she sends it on to someone else, that third person can easily learn the first person's e-mail address, even though the two people could be complete strangers to each other.

Sometimes unethical salespeople use e-mail chain letters to find out the e-mail addresses of the people who get the chain letter forwarded to them. Make sure friends know that they should not forward your e-mail messages to other people. You should not forward their e-mail messages, either. Be wary of sending e-mail chain letters to your friends, and ask them not to send you any, either.

Users can copy e-mail messages to a lot of people at one time by using the "cc" line. This means "carbon copy" and comes from the time when people used carbon paper to type copies of letters. They would type "cc" and then list all the people who would receive a copy of the letter. Using the cc line to send e-mail means that all the people

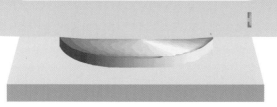

E-mail Dos and Don'ts

➢ Keep messages short.

➢ Use emoticons (characters grouped together to look like a certain emotion) sometimes, but not all the time.

➢ DON'T USE ALL CAPITALS! IT IS LIKE SHOUTING!

➢ Don't send junk mail.

➢ Don't send private messages.

➢ Don't mass-forward messages.

➢ Don't forward without permission from both the sender and the recipient.

Source: *Get Cybersavvy!*, n.d., 1998, <http://www.cybersavvy.org> (November 22, 1999).

who receive the e-mail message can see the e-mail addresses of all the other people who received the message. Request that your friends send you e-mail separately, not using the cc line. Some e-mail programs have a "blind copy" or "blind carbon copy" ("bc" or "bcc") line. This can be used to send an e-mail to many people without revealing their e-mail addresses to each other.

Users who post messages on a bulletin board or newsgroup or chat in a chat room can reveal their e-mail addresses to anyone else who visits the area. Once a user's e-mail address is known by others, several things can happen. The user might be constantly annoyed by sales ploys, scams, and advertisements. Armed with an e-mail address, a person can find out a street address or other information that strangers should not know. Finally, someone could send e-mail messages with threatening or offensive content.

Visiting a Web site can reveal personal information, too. Some Web sites use cookies, which are basically tracking devices that tell them about the people who visit their Web site. A cookie is a small program that gets transferred to the hard drive of a computer when a person visits a site. It identifies the person's computer when the person returns to the Web site that sent it. Cookies are generally used to track how well advertisements work and for general informational purposes, but the information they gather can be put to any use.[13] A user can be giving personal information to other people without even knowing about it. Some computer programs (like Web browsers) can disable cookies or alert users when they visit a site containing them.

Many Web sites will ask for visitors' e-mail addresses, usually in order to send product information. However, young people should ask permission from parents before sending any such information. Parents may want to make sure the site has a privacy policy before allowing their e-mail address to be shared.

Addiction and Social Isolation

Other people—and how they act—are not the only dangers of the Internet. Because it is so fascinating, people occasionally spend more time online than they should. They may be surfing the Internet when they should be doing other things. As noted computer expert and author Peter Kent points out, "I've heard stories of people getting stuck online for hours at a time, until early in the morning—or early in the morning after that".[14] One of the more common problems with the Internet is that people can easily spend too much time on it. Some people even develop an addiction—they become so accustomed to and dependent on Internet use that they have trouble giving it up or enjoying other activities. They spend so much time surfing that they do poorly in school, lose their jobs, or develop problems in their relationships with others. "There's just so much out there," Kent says, that "if you go on a voyage of discovery, you will find something interesting. . . . You can get so involved in the ongoing conversations that you can end up spending half your day just reading and responding."[15]

These problems can usually be solved by limiting the amount of time one spends on the computer. A timer or an alarm clock can be set as a reminder.

Also, one can call or visit people who live nearby instead of e-mailing them.

Hackers

Hackers are people who enjoy the challenge of entering other people's computer systems, often illegally. Sometimes they do it simply to know that they can. Sometimes they do it with malicious or criminal intent. Hackers can easily access information. They can create "Trojan Horse" programs, which appear to do one thing but actually perform a different task. For example, a hacker could create a fake log-in screen so that when users typed their passwords, the hacker would be able to collect them, then use the passwords later to access the other users' Internet accounts.[16]

*H*acker "Mudge" has boasted that he and fellow hackers could disable the entire Internet in thirty minutes because security is so poor. He is shown here on May 19, 1998, testifying before a Senate committee hearing on hacking.

Hackers can get into the records of online services and discover personal information. They can also use finger programs that retrieve information about other people on the Internet, even if all they have to go by is a username. A hacker who has a person's name can find out that person's address and phone number in seconds, using commonly available online databases. The Internet can even provide hackers with a map to a person's home, if they know the address.

If hackers have the right password, they have access to all the information in a person's computer, every document or record, even credit card numbers from purchases made over the Internet. Some people use sophisticated programs to keep hackers from tampering with their computers, but hackers seem to enjoy these challenges and can often find a way around any computer protection system.

Con Artists and Frauds

Con artists and frauds abound on the Internet. They advertise get-rich-quick schemes or work-at-home schemes. They offer "incredibly low prices" on products or have "hot deals" on illegally copied software. They offer weight-loss programs and "cures" for illnesses. Such offers sound too good to be true, and they often are. Recently, a fifteen-year-old boy posted an Internet advertisement selling computer equipment. Buyers sent money to him but received nothing in return. At the time of his arrest, he had stolen over ten thousand dollars without ever providing the buyers with a product or service.[17]

Con artists promise prizes and sweepstakes giveaways. "Just register to win!" they say. They ask for a credit card number so people can "claim a prize." Of course, the prize never arrives. Never give credit card information over the Internet without receiving permission first. Do not fall for this con.

Some con artists have even created fake Web sites using the names of real companies to get people to order merchandise with credit cards. The con artist has no intention of delivering anything in return.[18]

Dangerous and False Information, Pranks, and Hoaxes

Although the Web is full of good information, some of the information available on the Web is misleading, even dangerous. Rumors and lies are easily spread, with so many people communicating almost instantly with so many others. Unlike information published in books and magazines or broadcast on television, information on the Internet is not checked for facts. It is easy to be fooled, because people are used to public information being held to certain standards of truth and accuracy. When you use information from the Internet—for example, in a term paper—make sure the information comes from a reliable source, such as the Web sites of newspapers, encyclopedias, and magazines.

Some of the information on the Internet can be dangerous. People can find instructions for making bombs or drugs. They might be fooled into believing medical advice offered by someone who has no medical credentials.

Pranks and hoaxes also abound on the Internet. Chain letters get forwarded by the thousands every day. Some famous chain letters tell people that they will have good luck if they forward the e-mail message to ten friends. These types of e-mail messages are, of course, simply hoaxes. Hoaxes are usually less serious than actual fraud. To avoid these problems, even though they might not be too serious, do not respond to "urgent" messages from unknown people. Do not pass on chain letters, and do not believe everything you read on the Internet.

Unrestricted Marketing

Companies want people's money, and they will do just about anything to persuade people to give it to them. Advertising and selling on the Internet, unlike television and print advertising, is unregulated. Often it is difficult to tell the difference between the content of a Web site and its advertisements. Advertisers sometimes set up kids' sites and chat rooms just for sales purposes. They ask for personal information and track online use. They may offer free gifts to people who respond to their surveys. The advertisers may even personalize advertisements, according to what people tell them they like. Such pressure can be hard to resist.

This type of selling is called "permission marketing." It is popular among online companies. They believe people will appreciate personalized advertisements, so they ask for personal information. But do they really need to know everything about a customer's lifestyle and habits in order to sell that person something? One online sales consultant says, "A lot of these permission marketers are kind of greedy—they want to know too many things."[19] It is wise to ignore such sales attempts. Always refuse to give personal information.

Computer Viruses

Computer viruses can spread quickly throughout the Internet. A virus is a computer code created to cause problems in other people's computer systems. It can attach to computer files, duplicate itself, and destroy data or cause equipment malfunctions.

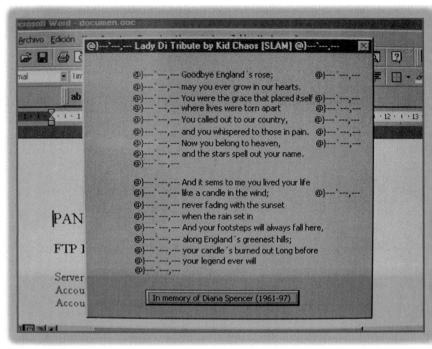

The Lady Diana computer virus filled affected computer screens in 1998 with verses from "Goodbye English Rose." This Elton John song was a tribute to the late princess.

Some viruses are pranks, and do not do any lasting harm. Others are malicious, usually intended for a specific target, such as an ex-employer. The target company then unknowingly spreads the virus by sharing files with other computers. Computer viruses have been spread through e-mail attachments and, in at least one case, the e-mail message itself. One destructive program, called a worm because it could get in a computer's hard drive and copy itself, randomly erased files from computers that were affected. The worm caused millions of dollars of damage to thousands of people's computers, interrupting business and disrupting communication among computer users.[20]

Downloading information from the Internet is never completely safe. There is always a chance that a virus could be downloaded. Be careful. Verify that the site is legitimate. Before you download anything, ask permission from parents. They may (and probably should) ask that all downloaded information be run through a virus-check program first. A virus-check program scans downloaded information and programs for viruses. If it detects a virus, it will alert the user. However, virus-check programs are not always reliable, because new viruses are being created every day. Therefore, computer users also have to remain cautious and use good judgment about downloading information.

Chapter 3

Surfing Safely: What Not to Do

The Internet is full of pitfalls and promises, just like the real world. However, it is complicated by the fact that people usually cannot see or hear the people that they meet. Web sites and chat rooms have no physical existence. This leads to special problems. Even though the Internet might not be as safe as people sometimes think, some precautions can help users avoid unpleasant happenings.

Do Not Give Out Personal Information

Never give out personal information on the Internet. Do not reveal your full name, address, school name, telephone number, or even local landmarks. Some Web sites ask for the user's name and address before allowing the person to enter. Instead of doing so, skip the Web site. Some people give a fake name and address, but it is better just to find another site to visit. Would a clothing store make you fill out a form before you could walk into the store? Of course not. Why should a Web site?

As one computer security expert says, "Would you give a stranger on the street your home address?"[1] It is smart to think of Web sites as strangers. Sites have sneaky ways of getting this information from people, though. They may ask visitors to fill out member lists or questionnaires. One kids' site reminds kids to keep personal information private, then says, "Passwords are used on the Internet for your protection. Choose a password that is easy for you to remember but hard for others to guess. What is your most frequently used password?" If you answer, the site says, "We fooled you! Remember, you should NEVER give out your password."[2]

Most Web sites are not trying to educate people, as that one is. They are trying to get information, sometimes for legitimate purposes, and sometimes not. Since no one can tell for certain how a site will use information—or if a hacker might get the information from the site without the owner's permission—the best thing to do is simply to never

Newsgroup Dos and Don'ts

✓Only post messages that are relevant.

✓Keep postings short.

✓Don't post personal messages.

✓Don't make insulting, degrading, offensive, or racist remarks.

*A*s vice president, Al Gore, shown here holding a brochure entitled "Parents Guide to the Internet," worked to make the Internet a safer place for young people.

give out personal information. It is very easy to get fooled into answering questions, especially when visiting sites that seem trustworthy.

Some Web sites offer prizes if users give them personal information. Even legitimate companies such as Nickelodeon and Disney do this, and almost half of all the kids they ask do respond.[3] One teen-oriented Web site asks for the name and e-mail address of a friend in exchange for a reward—so instead of asking people to reveal personal information about themselves, the Web site asks people to reveal personal information about their friends.[4] Never respond to these enticements and ask your friends to steer clear of them as well.

One kids' Web site puts it very bluntly: "Anything you disclose to us is ours. That's right—ours. So we can do anything we want with the stuff you post. We can reproduce it, disclose it, transmit it, publish it, broadcast it and post it someplace else. We can even send it to your mother (as soon as we find her address)."[5]

Besides personal information, never send personal pictures—or anything else personal—over the Internet without special permission from parents.[6]

Do Not Respond to Inappropriate Messages

Chantal, a teenager, is visiting a chat room when another person in the chat room suddenly sends her an obscene message. Her first reaction might be to tell the person who is harassing her to stop it and leave her alone, but that would only encourage the person's behavior. That is what the harasser wants—for Chantal to get upset and respond. Chantal's best bet is never to respond to inappropriate messages. It is not her fault if someone sends an inappropriate message, so she should not feel ashamed or embarrassed by it.

If something like this happens—you come across information or get messages that make you feel uncomfortable—always tell your parents. Alert them so that they can take steps to keep your Internet experience enjoyable and rewarding.

Remember, just because someone wants to talk, you do not have to respond. Like Chantal, if you are in a chat room and someone demands your attention, you can ignore that person. If someone makes you uncomfortable, stop talking. You do not have to have any other reason.[7]

Internet Safety Quiz

Which of the following pieces of information should you NOT give on the Internet without your parents' permission?

➤ First name
➤ Last name
➤ Age
➤ Birthday
➤ Home address
➤ Phone number

➤ Parent's name
➤ City
➤ Hobbies
➤ E-mail address
➤ School name

Answer: You should not give out ANY of the above pieces of information without your parents' permission.

Do Not Send Inappropriate Messages

Greg, a teenager, is playing an online computer game with several other people. They are having a great time and seem to be winning. Then a person who is on Greg's side turns around and kills Greg's character. Nothing can make computer gamers as mad as that. Without thinking, Greg might type a mean message on the screen. Or because he knows the other player's e-mail address, he might send a note saying how much he hates playing with people who do that. Greg thinks that is the end of it. But then the other player responds with a threatening message, something that scares Greg. What now?

Greg is too embarrassed by the threatening message to show it to his parents, since he sent a mean message in the first place. But Greg should show his parents, even if they might not be pleased with his behavior. Getting hateful or threatening messages happens more than most people realize. In computer lingo, it is called "getting flamed." There is nothing funny about it. It can be frightening.[8]

Of course, one way to help keep this from happening is to not send inappropriate messages. Although Greg was really mad at the other player, he should have stepped away from the computer and cooled off. If the other player ever wanted to join a game again, Greg could refuse, saying he does not like to play with "player-killers." He should not send nasty notes, though. As Robert B. Gelman, an Internet and computer systems expert, says, "If you wouldn't like your Mom to read what you've written, consider rewriting it."[9]

In chat rooms, the rules of public conversation

Emoticons

Internet users use emoticons to help express themselves in an e-mail message. Because e-mail messages can be misunderstood, a person can use an emoticon to show he or she is joking or to say that he or she is upset.

Tilt the page on its side to see what these emoticons look like.

:-)	smile	:D	big smile or laugh	:*	kiss
;)	wink	:X	keep a secret	:(	frown
:'(	crying	:O	surprised	:I	bored
:>	silly grin	8-)	feeling goofy	:&	do not know what to say
{}	hug	{{}}	big hug	::	wave
O:)	angel	}:>	devil	:-P	sticking tongue out

apply. This means that people should not discuss things they would not discuss in a shopping mall where everyone else could overhear what they are saying. Do not say things that would make you (or the people you care about, such as your parents) uncomfortable if a stranger heard them. Remember that even if you think only you and another person are in a chat room, other people can monitor chat groups without revealing their presence.[10]

Patricia sent an e-mail to her friend Stacy, telling her how Stacy had hurt her feelings. Patricia wanted her friend to know that she had been disappointed in her behavior and wanted to find out if she had done something to cause it. However, Stacy's father happened to check the family's e-mail messages first, and he read Patricia's note. Although he would never have opened a letter addressed to Stacy, when the e-mail message popped up, he read it. Then, he was upset. He told Stacy not to answer Patricia because he did not think she should have insulted Stacy. Although Patricia just wanted to share her feelings, her message was misunderstood by Stacy's father. It is easy for this to happen with written messages. This misunderstanding made it difficult for Stacy and Patricia to remain friends. Now Patricia wishes she had made an extra effort to talk to Stacy at school or at least call her on the telephone so they could have talked in private. Patricia found out the hard way that e-mail messages can easily be seen and read by the wrong people.[11]

Computer expert and author Peter Kent says, "The more I use e-mail, the more I believe it can be a dangerous tool. There are three main problems: 1) people often don't realize the implications of what

Chat Room Dos and Don'ts

✓ Say hello so people know you are there.

✓ Use a nickname.

✓ Use abbreviations sparingly.

✓ Make sure your message cannot be misinterpreted or misunderstood.

✓ Don't use capital letters.

✓ Don't try to get attention by drawing attention to yourself.

✓ Don't give personal information.

they're saying, 2) People often misinterpret what others are saying and 3) People are comfortable typing things into a computer that they would never say to a person face-to-face. Consequently, online fights are common."[12]

Court cases have shown that judges do not believe e-mail communications are private or should be protected by privacy laws. This is especially true of e-mail accounts that employers provide to workers. The same applies to e-mail people might send or receive from school or the library. Not only could the boss or teacher monitor the e-mail, many other people could see it on the way to its destination, and even after it has reached its destination.[13]

For these reasons, it is very important to think carefully before sending an e-mail or posting a message to a bulletin board. Never send inappropriate messages, and think about how your words could be interpreted.

Never Arrange Meetings

Finally, and most important, to guard against physical danger, never put yourself in a dangerous position. Sometimes people on the Internet seem like interesting friends who have the same hobbies and interests. One or two Internet friends might even want to arrange a meeting in person. You might be tempted, especially if you seem to have a lot in common.

Because it is impossible to tell if people on the Internet are who they say they are, never arrange face-to-face meetings with them. Although it might happen in the movies or in a story, never do it in real life. If someone asks to meet you, refuse and tell your parents about it right away.

Chapter 4

Surfing Safely: What to Do

There are many things you should not do on the Internet, but there are some things you should do to make your experience as safe and enjoyable as possible.

Leave Unsafe Sites Immediately

If you are surfing on the Internet and you come across obscene or frightening material, leave the site immediately. Click on the Home icon or close the browser right away. Tell your parents what happened so that they can help you avoid such sites in the future and so that they can take action if necessary.[1]

Marsha, a computer whiz, remembers when she first started using the Internet. She would use a search engine to look up keywords such as "girl" or "toys" and was sometimes surprised at the kinds of things that turned up.[2] She points out that you can end up looking at a Web site that you never wanted to see. "Just one click and you're out of there!" she says.

Select Neutral Names and Addresses

If you can, choose an e-mail address that does not reveal personal information. Many professional people have e-mail addresses that start with their last name for business reasons. However, most people, especially children and young adults, should use e-mail addresses that do not give personal information.

In chat rooms, newsgroups, bulletin boards, and among online gamers, choose a name that does not reveal your identity. Use just initials or a gender-neutral name or something completely unrelated, such as "rain cloud." This prevents people from finding out more about you. Such precautions can often help prevent girls from getting unwanted messages; some Internet users think it is funny to send obscene messages to teenage girls. People should not be able to identify you by the name you use or the e-mail address you give.[3]

To join a chat group, leave a question on a bulletin-board service, or have a Web site send information, give out an e-mail address only. Ask your parents for their permission first, because they may prefer that you not give the e-mail address at all.[4]

Educate Others

If you have younger brothers and sisters, you should educate them about surfing the Internet safely. Ask older siblings for their ideas on visiting the Internet without having any bad experiences. Ask them about using the Internet for fun. If they do not know as much about the Internet as you do, go online

Keep the Rules of the Internet Posted Near Your Computer

✓ Observe others who act correctly online to learn how they behave.

✓ Remember to think of the other person's feelings.

✓ Be courteous when you ask for help or complain about the behavior of others.

✓ Watch what you say about other people.

✓ Keep communications short and to the point.

✓ Check your spelling.

✓ Clearly indicate the subject of your e-mail or posting.

✓ Do not forget your audience.

✓ Use humor and sarcasm with care.

✓ Do not repeat messages.

✓ Credit sources of information.

✓ Tolerate the mistakes of others.

✓ Do not send or display offensive messages or pictures.

✓ Do not use obscene language.

✓ Never harass or insult others.

Source: Lawrence Magid, *SafeKids.Com*, 1998, <http://www.safekids.com> (November 22, 1999).

*T*he Internet can be a vast resource for students. Teens can use it to learn more about the government, and even to contact the White House at http://www.whitehouse.org.

together and give them pointers. You can do the same for friends.

You may even know more than your parents do about the Internet. If so, share what you know and show them the ropes so that they can safely enjoy the Internet along with you. Pooling resources can help everyone learn more about Internet safety.[5]

Protect Privacy

People can visit an anonymizer or use a remailer Web site to maintain their privacy. But this step is unnecessary if you remember to think before you act. Always ask your parents before you respond to e-mails or requests for information if you are not sure what to do or how to handle a certain situation.

To protect your privacy, your parents may not want you to visit open or public chat rooms, where anyone interested can join the conversation. Ask them if you can create a private chat room, giving the password to select friends and family members.[6] Think of other creative ways to enjoy everything the Internet has to offer without sacrificing privacy.

Set Ground Rules

Cooperate with your parents in setting ground rules. Everyone should have clear expectations regarding when you can go online, how long you can stay online, and what you can do online. Your parents may not want you to join chat groups, or they may want you to tell them whenever you are going online. They may want you to go online only when they are home to help you. Make sure you know what the family rules are. Post them next to the computer. Then remember to abide by them.[7]

Respect Parents' Wishes

Respect the family Internet rules if you go online at school or the library. If your parents do not want you to join chat groups from the computer at home, you can bet they do not want you to join them from the computer at school. If your teacher or school has special guidelines for Internet use (for instance, only for research), then you must respect that as well.

Sometimes parents invest in blocking or filtering devices to help you avoid inappropriate sites. Some of the blocking devices simply refuse access to sites with certain words in the name, such as "drugs" or "sex." Then even if you wanted to know more about

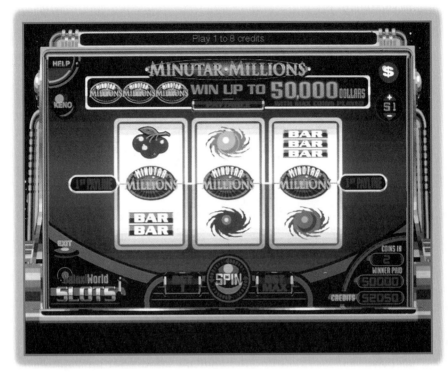

*A*lthough Internet surfers can explore many educational and recreational Web sites, there are some areas, such as gambling sites, that are negative influences on teens.

a topic such as sexual harassment, you might not be able to access the site. Other blocking devices block specific sites that are listed on an "unsafe Web sites" list. The list of sites is updated by computer users as they find sites inappropriate for children. These blocking devices require more effort to maintain but tend to be better at blocking only inappropriate sites instead of all sites on a general subject. Other programs use ranking services to allow access to approved Web sites.[8]

Blocking programs can prevent users from sending e-mail or providing personal information.[9]

Some of this software allows online monitoring so that your parents (or an employer) can see where their children (or employees) have been on the Internet.[10] Some Internet Service Providers also provide blocking programs for users.

Blocking or filtering devices can be used for other helpful purposes. For instance, if someone is sending e-mail messages that you do not want to receive, you can use a filtering device to prevent the messages from being sent to you from a particular e-mail address.

If your parents invest in this type of equipment or software, respect their decision. Parents who use such devices are trying to make surfing the Internet a safe and enjoyable experience for you without having to supervise every second of your time online. If you feel that this means your parents do not trust you, do not try to get around the blocking device or go to a friend's house to use his or her computer. Instead, discuss it with your parents. Tell them how you feel and listen closely to their reasons for using this device.

Enjoy the Experience

The Internet is an entertaining, fascinating world to visit. When you are there, remember to use good judgment and critical thinking skills at all times. If you follow the proper safety guidelines, you will be able to keep your visits to the world of the Internet safe and enjoyable.

Organizations

Child Lures
5166 Shelburne Road
Shelburne, VT 05482
(802) 985-8458
<http://www.childlures.com>

Children's Partnership
1351 Third Street Promenade, Suite 206
Santa Monica, CA 90401-1321
(310) 260-1220
<http://www.childrenspartnership.org>

Children's Safety Network
55 Chapel Street
Newton, MA 02458-1060
(617) 969-7101, ext. 2207
<http://www.edc.org/HHD/csn>

Web Sites

America Links Up
<http://www.americalinksup.org>

Don't Spread that Hoax!
<http://www.nonprofit.net/hoax>

FBI Kids & Youth Educational Page
<http://www.fbi.gov/kids/kids.htm>

Get Cyber Savvy!
<http://www.cybersavvy.org>

National Center for Missing and Exploited Children
<http://www.missingkids.com>

SafeKids.Com
<http://www.safekids.com>

SafeSurf®
<http://www.safesurf.com>

SafeTeens.Com
<http://www.safeteens.com>

Web Wise Kids™
<http://www.webwisekids.com>

If you have problems while surfing the Internet, tell your parents right away. Obscene material or threatening messages should be handled by a person in authority. To report problems or get help, call your Internet Service Provider and explain the situation (you can usually access its Web page and get reporting information by going to <www.serviceprovider.com>. Depending on the problem, your service provider can often help you stop inappropriate communications. It can withdraw a person's online privileges, for example. If someone sends a threatening message or commits some sort of crime, such as fraud, using the computer, you (with your parents) should report it to the local law enforcement agency. Here are some other organizations that can help with problems on the Internet.

➤ You can also report problems and get help from CyberTipline, sponsored by the National Center for Missing and Exploited Children at <www.missingkids.com/cybertip>. Or call 1-800-843-5678.

➤ The Child Pornography Tipline: 1-800-843-5678.

➤ The National Fraud Information Center sponsors Internet Fraud Watch. Report suspicious or illegal activities at <www.fraud.org> or 1-800-876-7060. Its mailing address is P.O. Box 65868, Washington, D.C. 20035.

➤ The Computer Emergency Response Team handles security breaches. It can be

Where to Find Help

reached at the CERT Coordination Center
<cert@cert.org> or 412-268-7090.

➤ The Federal Bureau of Investigation is
responsible for computer crimes that are
against federal laws: National Computer
Crime Squad, Tenth and Pennsylvania
Avenue, Washington, D.C. 20535. Telephone: 202-324-3283. You can visit its
Web site at <www.fbi.gov>.

➤ The Federal Trade Commission Bureau
of Consumer Protection has a Web site
with information on Internet marketing
practices: <www.ftc.gov>. To register a
complaint, e-mail <consumerline@ftc.gov>
or telephone 202-326-3128.

Introduction

1. "Ohio Man Pleads Guilty to Enticing New Jersey Girl," Office of the U.S. Attorney for the District of New Jersey, press release, June 23, 1997.

Chapter 1. What Is the Internet?

1. *World Almanac and Book of Facts* (Mahwah, N.J., World Almanac Books, 1998), p. 643.

2. Chris Peterson, *I Love the Internet but I Want My Privacy, Too!* (Rocklin, Calif.: Prima Publishing, 1998), p. 7.

3. Galen Grimes, *The Ten Minute Guide to the Internet and World Wide Web* (Indianapolis: Que Corporation, 1997), pp. 5–8.

4. Peter Kent, *The Complete Idiot's Guide to the Internet* (Indianapolis: Que Corporation, 1998), pp. 124, 151.

5. Grimes, p. 11.

6. Teacher Created Materials, Inc., *Internet for Kids* (Huntington Beach, Calif.: Teacher Created Materials, Inc., 1996), p. 22.

7. Kent, p. 63.

8. World Almanac and Book of Facts, p. 643.

9. Peterson, p. 42.

10. Kent, p. 22.

11. Peterson, p. 42.

12. Lawrence J. Magid, "Parents' Guide to the Internet," fact sheet, National Center for Missing and Exploited Children, 1998.

Chapter 2. How Can the Internet Be Unsafe?

1. Laura E. Quarantiello, *CyberCrime: How to Protect Yourself from Computer Criminals* (Lake Geneva, Wis.: Limelight Books, 1997), p. 37.

2. Chris Peterson, *I Love the Internet but I Want My Privacy, Too!* (Rocklin, Calif.: Prima Publishing, 1998), pp. 97–98.

3. "Latest Web Statistics," *Web Police*, March 1, 1999, <www.web-police.org> (April 13, 1999.)

4. *World Almanac and Book of Facts* (Mahwah, N.J.: World Almanac Books, 1998), p. 644.

5. Ibid.

6. Peter Kent, *The Complete Idiot's Guide to the Internet* (Indianapolis: Que Corporation, 1998), p. 257.

7. Lawrence J. Magid, "Teen Safety on the Information Highway," National Center for Missing and Exploited Children, 1998, p. 7.

8. Peterson, p. 39.

9. Kent, p. 248.

10. Quarantiello, p. 61.

11. Ibid., p. 166.

12. Angie Cannon and Warren Cohen, "The Church of the Almighty White Man," *US News and World Report*, July 19, 1999, p. 22.

13. Kent, p. 249.

14. Ibid., p. 253.

15. Ibid.

16. Brendan Koerner, "Can Hackers Be Stopped?" *US News and World Report*, June 14, 1999, p. 52.

17. Quarantiello, p. 73.

18. Peterson, p. 69.

19. "Marketing: I Will If You Will," *Wired*, May 1999, p. 74.

20. "Worm with an Attitude," *US News and World Report*, June 28, 1999, p. 53.

Chapter 3. Surfing Safely: What Not to Do

1. Laura E. Quarantiello, *CyberCrime: How to Protect Yourself from Computer Criminals* (Lake Geneva, Wis.: Limelight Books, 1997), p. 96.

2. "Get Your Web License," *PBS Kids* n.d., <http://www.pbs.org/kids> (October 20, 1998).

3. Chris Peterson, *I Love the Internet but I Want My Privacy, Too!* (Rocklin, Calif.: Prima Publishing, 1998), p. 103.

4. Ibid., p. 106.

5. Center for Media Education, "The Deceiving Web of Online Advertising," fact sheet, 1998.

6. Quarantiello, p. 100.

7. Peterson, p. 75.

8. Peter Kent, *The Complete Idiot's Guide to the Internet* (Indianapolis: Que Corporation, 1998), p. 269.

9. Robert B. Gelman and the Electronic Frontier Foundation, *Protecting Yourself Online* (New York: HarperCollins, 1998), p. 29.

10. Peterson, p. 75

11. Kent, p. 35.

12. Ibid, p. 34.

13. Peterson, p. 61.

Chapter 4. Surfing Safely: What to Do

1. Lawrence J. Magid, "Teen Safety on the Information Highway," National Center for Missing and Exploited Children, 1998, p. 5.

2. Ann Orr, "Cyber-Safety," *Working Mother*, May 1998, p. 54.

3. Chris Peterson, *I Love the Internet but I Want My Privacy, Too!* (Rocklin, Calif.: Prima Publishing, 1998), p. 42.

4. Ibid.

5. Magid, p. 12.

6. Orr, p. 57.

7. Ibid., p. 54.

8. Ibid., p. 55.

9. Peter Kent, *The Complete Idiot's Guide to the Internet* (Indianapolis: Que Corporation, 1998), p. 249.

10. Robert B. Gelman and the Electronic Frontier Foundation, *Protecting Yourself Online* (New York: HarperCollins, 1998), p. 67.

address—The special location of information on the Internet, such as a Web page or e-mail user.

anonymizer sites—Sites where people can go to get anonymous user IDs, so information cannot be collected about them.

browser—A program that lets you view information on the Web, such as Web pages.

bulletin-board service—A network of computers that can be dialed up separately from the Internet. Members post and read messages. Computer companies often use these services to post technical information and programs that users can download to fix problems.

chat rooms—Places on the Internet where people can meet and talk with each other in real time. They cannot post messages and return later to see if there have been any responses.

cookie—A small program that is transferred to a computer's hard drive when certain Web sites are visited. The cookie contains information so that when a site is revisited, it recognizes the computer again. Cookies can also track online movements.

domain—The address of a company or organization with a Web site.

download—To copy a file from one computer to another.

e-mail (electronic mail)—A method of sending written messages from one computer to another, usually over a modem and phone line.

flame—A nasty e-mail message or posting in a newsgroup, bulletin board, or chat room.

going online—Using the Internet.

Internet—An worldwide network of computer networks that allows people to communicate with each other and share information.

Internet Service Provider (ISP)—A company that offers Internet access.

modem—A computer accessory that converts digital data from your computer to analog signals so that they can be transmitted over the phone lines. Cable and other types of modems or adapters format digital data to be transmitted over various types of lines.

netiquette—Guidelines for interacting with other people on the Internet.

newsgroup—One of thousands of special interest groups that computer users can join to talk about topics of interest. Users post and respond to messages.

remailer—A service that will remove a user's identifying information before an e-mail is sent.

search engine—A site that allows computer users to find information on the Internet by entering keywords.

Uniform Resource Locator (URL)—The address of a page on the World Wide Web.

virus—A computer program that causes unexpected and unwanted problems such as damaged data. Viruses can be transmitted by downloading programs from the Internet or can be present on a disk that came from an infected computer.

World Wide Web—The part of the Internet that presents information in language and images that users can understand.

Cochrane, Kerry. *The Internet*. New York: Franklin Watts, 1995.

Gelman, Robert B., and the Electronic Frontier Foundation. *Protecting Yourself Online*. New York: HarperCollins, 1998.

Grimes, Galen. *The Ten Minute Guide to the Internet and World Wide Web*. Indianapolis: Que Corporation, 1997.

Kent, Peter. *The Complete Idiot's Guide to the Internet*. Fifth edition. Indianapolis: Que Corporation, 1998.

Magid, Lawrence. *The Little PC Book*. Berkeley, Calif.: Peach Pit Press, 1999.

McCormick, Anita Louise. *The Internet: Surfing the Issues*. Springfield, N.J.: Enslow Publishers, 1998.

Peterson, Chris. *I Love the Internet but I Want My Privacy, Too!* Rocklin, Calif.: Prima Publishing, 1998.

Quarantiello, Laura E. *How to Protect Yourself from Computer Criminals*. Lake Geneva, Wis.: Limelight Books, 1997.

Teacher Created Materials, Inc. *Internet for Kids*. Huntington Beach, Calif.: Teacher Created Materials, Inc., 1996.